BREATH, WATER, LIGHT

Simple Tools for Creating Inner Peace

Anna Ashe

Order this book online at www.trafford.com
or email orders@trafford.com

Most Trafford titles are also available at major online book retailers.

© Copyright 2010 Anna Ashe.
All rights reserved. No part of this publication may be reproduced, stored
in a retrieval system, or transmitted, in any form or by any means, electronic,
mechanical, photocopying, recording, or otherwise, without
the written prior permission of the author.

Printed in Victoria, BC, Canada.

ISBN: 978-1-4269-2423-1

*Our mission is to efficiently provide the world's finest, most
comprehensive book publishing service, enabling every author to
experience success. To find out how to publish your book, your way, and
have it available worldwide, visit us online at www.trafford.com*

Trafford rev. 1/20/2010

Trafford PUBLISHING www.trafford.com

North America & international
toll-free: 1 888 232 4444 (USA & Canada)
phone: 250 383 6864 ♦ fax: 812 355 4082

Peace within
is like a ripple of water,
it starts from the
centre
of our being
and
flows out in all directions
into the universe
radiating kindness
and love
from our hearts
into the heart of all
living beings.

Medical Disclaimer

The information in this book is not intended or implied to be substitute for professional medical advice, diagnosis or treatment. The information provided in this book is for the general information of the reader and should not be considered professional medical advice. Please consult with your physician if you have health concerns, especially with the breathing exercises as these may cause hyper-ventilation in some people. Readers assume responsibility for the use of any information provided herein.

BREATH, WATER, LIGHT

I breathe, I live.
I drink, I am refreshed.
I love, I shine.

Introduction

Breath, water and light are three core tools that I use for creating a sense of peace within myself. My theory is that if enough individuals focus on creating peace within their own hearts, minds and bodies, a peaceful world will be a natural result.

I have experienced a profound sense of peace and unconditional love that I would like to share with you. Contained in this book are examples and exercises that I have found most powerful. I like to believe that I am not special and that anyone with the intent of creating peace and accepting unconditional love has the power to do it themselves.

Having this knowledge has not created peace in all of my moments, nor has it turned me into a saint. I have held off writing this book for many years, waiting for all the parts of myself to grow up, wake up, make up… in essence, waiting for perfection. Still, I find myself in stressful and heart-breaking situations, often of my own creation. What never leaves me though, even in my darkest moments, is the knowing in my heart that peace exists, and it is mine for the choosing. Perfection has eluded me but my trust in and my connection to this state of inner peace remains intact.

Do you want this kind of knowing, this kind of feeling?

Would you like to take more control and be more aware of your energy levels?

Are you courageous enough to look inside your own mind, body and heart and seek out areas where you have been hurt in the past and take control of your own healing?

Are you ready to feel more joy in your everyday existence?

If your answer to each of the above questions is yes, I hope that the tools that I am sharing in this handbook empower you to create your own sense of peace.

INTENTION
and
WILLINGNESS

Reaching and experiencing your own inner peace starts with clearly stating this as your sincere intention. Willingness is the energy of accepting the changes and challenges that will come with connecting more fully to your self. As you move through the exercises in this book, you may experience feelings of resistance and fear. It is your willingness that overcomes the resistance. If you start feeling overwhelmed, just re-state that even with all the shadows of doubt and fear surrounding you, experiencing a feeling of peace is your goal and your intention.

Each exercise in this book has the potential to create a shift or change in your being. Choosing peace may create temporary chaos in your life so I advise that you work with the exercises in moderation using your own intuition as a guide. There is no order of importance. Your attention will be drawn to the exercises that will best serve you in the moment.

Self-healing will most likely create waves in the relationships that are attached to you.

For example, if you are the needy one in a relationship, your loved one is used to this need and most likely associates it with love. Once you start a breathing routine, you may need less energy from your loved one and in turn, your loved one may feel less loved. Many people get a feeling of safety from being needed and for this reason it can become a controlling behavior. Hopefully, your loved one will also choose to find his/her own path to peace along with you and you can share the joys of discovery together.

On the other side of the coin, if you are the energy giver in your relationship and you start channeling more energy into your self instead of giving it to those around you, you may find your self on the receiving end of some unpleasant life reviews. Don't lose heart; those that truly love you will eventually adjust to the new you and even though it might not seem like it, you will open the doorway for others to heal and empower themselves.

As you are healing your self, try to tackle every situation with kindness and compassion. I believe that the present was directed and created by our actions and thoughts of the past. So try to live gracefully through any tragedies that you have created with your prior set of thoughts and intentions.

Your path to peace will be as unique as you are. Trust that goodness does exist within your heart, and that you are worthy of peace and unconditional love. I believe every individual that chooses to find his or her own path to inner peace eases the journey for those that come after them. It is the journey of a true hero.

Who Am I?

My name is Anna. I am 45 years old and the mother of three children. I have a career, a love-life, and hobbies, much like many other people in North America. When I was 29 years old, I had an experience that turned my world upside-down, or right-side-up, depending on how you look at it. At the time, I was working full-time. The ages of my children were five, four and one. I was tired, really tired.

For most of my life, I have been a philosopher and have questioned the purpose of life and the reasons for the pain and suffering that exists. Although my life had most of the elements of what was considered a good life, I felt emptiness. It seemed I had two lives, one was my life of thoughts and the other was the life I lived. Occasionally, I was able to share my thoughts and my two worlds joined. In those moments, I escaped the emptiness and felt for a few moments my true nature.

I realized that most of the people close to me didn't know or care to know my thoughts. I had spent most of my life trying to make myself acceptable to others and not make waves by questioning the status quo. When I looked at the outside world, I saw the faces of the hungry and the battered, the inequalities and distrust between men and women, and questioned the rightness of the saying 'mind your own business'. I asked myself whether peace was possible in this world. Was there anything I could do to help design a peaceful world?

Going to help out in troubled nations wasn't an option. I was already over my head with three children and the responsibility of caring for them, feeding them and putting a roof over their heads. Because I didn't have the time or energy to do great deeds outside of my own situation, I decided to experiment with ideas for creating peace within myself.

It was at this time, when I was passionately questioning my life, that people and experiences started coming to me. I went to see an energy healer who performed a healing technique that corrected my connection to what she called my higher self (or soul self), the part of me that is connected to all that is. It seemed as though my passionate thinking self took a step forward and faced the world full on. There are not words enough to describe the impact this event had on my perceptions, but I will try my best to give you an understanding of my experience.

Imagine that your body is a vehicle and you are a form of intelligent energy that drives the vehicle. Imagine the vehicle that you are driving in is a car. You have protection from the wind and the rain. You have temperature control and the ability to choose your driving speed. On occasion, you can roll down the windows and let the outside in, but for the most part you stay enclosed in a 'safe' place. Now, imagine that you are driving a motorcycle. There is nothing between you and the outside world. Paying attention to what is around becomes much more important and meaningful. It is a rush and heightening of sensation.

I remember walking down the street afterwards and being awed by the trees. Of course I had seen trees before, but I had never felt connected and close to them. Even the experience of my body took on a new meaning. All of a sudden, I could feel every movement my body made. I was dizzy from the thought that I had hands and those hands would do whatever I told them to.

The most amazing thing to me was that I hadn't realized previously that I was disconnected and operating my life from a distance. I can see clearly now that I had been living life mostly in my thoughts and only occasionally connecting to my body. From that point on, I could no longer avoid experiencing how situations affected my physical and emotional state of being.

So, with my desire to find peace within and the increased awareness of my physical and emotional state, I started studying, imagining, investigating and practicing different techniques for healing and for creating and maintaining a state of inner peace within myself. I set up rules and guidelines for what could go into my toolkit, the first and most important rule being that the tools I used must be accessible to everyone.

Because I had no idea what would make me feel contented, I surrendered to a higher power with the intention of wanting for myself only what was in the highest good of all concerned. I followed my intuition or inner-knowing as a guide for making life changing decisions, even if logically it didn't seem to make sense. I paid attention to my emotions and body-responses, especially those that caused me to feel uneasy and unwell. I paid more attention to the thoughts that entered my mind. I chose to believe in the thoughts that promoted a peaceful feeling within myself and let the other thoughts go with as minimal a struggle as I could master.

The work of healing one's self is endless, but I feel like I am a hero. I measure my progress in baby steps and continue to learn and strengthen. I could write pages and pages on the wonderful experiences that came my way once I surrendered to a higher power and started following my intuition. When I look back on my journey, I could cry with appreciation for the people and experiences that came my way to help me learn or to share their healing gifts with me.

I believe if you make a commitment to creating peace within yourself, and you are willing to accept good things, with the intention of wanting only what is in the highest good of all concerned, you open a doorway to receive goodness and to bask in the warmth of unconditional love. It is my hope that you will also be blessed in your journey as I have been. You deserve it.

NEVER UNDERESTIMATE THE POWER OF ONE DEEP BREATH.
NEVER UNDERESTIMATE THE POWER OF ONE DEEP BREATH.
NEVER UNDERESTIMATE THE POWER OF ONE DEEP BREATH.

BREATH

Peaceful Stillness

Breath is the tool I use to refuel my tired body with oxygen. I use it to clear my emotional state of negative thinking. I use it to connect to my soul self, the part of me that watches without judging, the part of me that sits in stillness at the centre of my being.

I like to think about breathing. It is one thing all human beings have in common. Breathing is an experience we all share. It is the one basic activity that keeps our bodies alive, in preparation and continuation of the experience of Life.

Human beings are programmed to breathe. We are compelled to breathe; it happens without our thinking about it. We are compelled to live, whether we want to or not. Unless we take our own life or our hearts fail, we do not have choice in this matter.

One area where we have freedom of choice is in how we use our breath. We can hold our breath or take slow deep breaths or just leave breathing to our automatic pilots, just as some examples for a start. It's your choice.

You are the boss of your breathing. You are the boss of your thinking. The rule and the challenge: You must breathe to live. You must live. How you choose to do either is up to you. You are the boss.

Being conscious of your breath will return you to your centre. Conscious breathing, that is, paying attention to the FEELING of your breath entering and exiting your body, allows for some space between the thoughts that move through your mind. In that space, you can catch a glimpse or a feeling of who you truly are behind all the mental programming and external qualities that you have attributed to your self.

I feel peaceful when I breathe consciously…centered, reflective, aware, alive. It gives me energy. The energy I get from breathing is energy that I don't need to take from the world around me. All of my senses are heightened when I breathe consciously, feeling what the air feels like, entering and exiting my body. I feel good. I feel content.

EXERCISES

Exercise 1: 10 Conscious Breaths

Purpose: I use this exercise to maintain or refuel my energy level and to reconnect my awareness to my physical body.

Timing/Duration: Try to do this every hour or every other hour throughout the day from waking until sleeping.

Step by Step Instructions:

1. Stop whatever you are doing.

2. Take 10 conscious breaths focusing your attention on the air entering and exiting the body.

    a. It can be a long deep breath or short breaths. The objective is to pay attention to your breath without letting your mind wander off into other areas of thought throughout the exercise.

    b. Breathe in through your nose and exhale either through your nose or mouth, whatever works for you.

    c. Pause slightly in between every inhale and exhale, and pay attention to the feeling in this space.

Notes/Comments: This sounds deceptively simple but, in reality, keeping to it is very difficult. I have rarely made it through a whole day doing this, but still, I try my best and when I do this, I feel rejuvenated.

Exercise 2: The Healing Breath

Purpose: I use this exercise periodically to clear toxins from my body. When I am feeling unwell, I use it to restore physical health to my body.

Timing/Duration: Once daily for fifteen minutes. Let your own sense of physical well-being be your guide as to when it is needed and for how long.

Step by Step Instructions:

1. Lie down in a comfortable position.

2. Breathe in deeply through your nose and hold your breath for 15 seconds or for as long as you can manage.

3. Evenly exhale all your breath prior to inhaling again.

4. Each time you take a new breath in, direct it to a part of your body. Work your way through your body in any way that amuses you. Use your imagination. The important thing to remember is not to leave out any parts of your body. If you are tempted to leave out parts of your body, pay special attention. This is usually where you need to heal the most.

5. After each part of your body has been addressed, imagine the breath filling your whole body, and imagine all your aches and pains leaving with the out-breath.

6. Lastly, fill your body with breath one more time, this time imagining joyful energy filling your whole body. On the out-breath, imagine this joyful energy surrounding you inside and out.

Notes/Comments: It may take some practice to make it through all parts of your body. I often focus on one part of my body for the whole fifteen minutes if it is causing me a lot of discomfort.

Breath, Water, Light

Exercise 3: The Clearing Breath

Purpose: This breathing exercise is one that I use to release negative emotional energy that has built up inside me. I use it to clear the space around me and within me of negative energy that I have picked up during the day. After doing this exercise, I feel much more grounded, centered and emotionally strong.

Timing/Duration: Daily or as needed.

Step by Step Instructions:

1. Sit or lie down in a comfortable position.

2. Focus your intention on clearing negativity with each breath, inside you and around you. Take a long breath deep into your stomach. Let the breath out slowly through the mouth with a long sighing sound….AUHHHHHHH. Try to make the AUH sound from as deep in your throat as you can.

3. I often do four of these breaths, one for each geographical direction (north, south, east, west), imagining any negative energies being blown out of the space surrounding me.

4. Imagine the negative energies turning to dust and you sweeping them up and putting them in the trash.

Exercise 4: The Fish Breath

Purpose: This technique may be helpful for those of you who have trouble breathing in through your nose. I use it when I have a stuffy nose. This is a great tool for getting breath deeper into your stomach as well.

Step by Step Instructions:

1. Imagine that you have two gills on either side of you throat.

2. While keeping your mouth closed, imagine the air coming in through these gills, and filling your lungs and stomach cavity.

The wind moves over the land
its source unknown.
The current flows through the water
its source unknown.

The wind moves over the land
The current flows through the water
Their source unknown.

We sleep and we wake
and truly
our lives are filled
with more mystery
than reality.

WATER

Peaceful Movement

Water is the tool I use to cleanse my body of toxins, both internally and externally. I use it to moderate my emotions. It is a powerful metaphor for an endless number of visualizations that help me manage my thoughts and connect more fully to the joy that exists in movement.

Thinking about water connects me to the earth. It seems to me to be the essence of life itself. Where breath and thought may be the winds and the currents of life, water is the substance that contains, sustains and expresses life. I am in awe of the myriad forms that it takes and by its movements from deep inside the earth to the streams and oceans and finally gathering above us in the skies and returning itself back to us.

Cold, clean water, so refreshing… warm, swirling water, so relaxing…BLISS.

Is there anyone on the earth that is not aware of the need for adequate water in order for our bodies to survive, in order for plants to grow? After breath, it is the next essential ingredient for life to survive. Still, many of us drink water unconsciously and for those of us in water rich nations, water is used without a thought for bathing, cleaning and cooking.

Being conscious of water intake is the first step in balancing out the elements in our bodies, and regaining a sense of comfort inside our bodies. Combined with breath, it is an essential building block to taking responsibility for the health of our selves. To our overall state of being, the awareness and appreciation of water reinforces within our hearts a sense of wealth of existence. When we are aware of our own wealth, we become more generous and less negative.

Our physical bodies are what connect us to the earth, being of the earth and sustained by elements provided by the earth. I believe that our emotional bodies are connected to our physical bodies and that emotional distress is the root of the lack of peace in our lives and in our world.

Emotions speak to us through our bodies; this is why it is so important to be connected to our physical sensations. No one calls hunger an emotion, but I have found through observation of my own emotional state that hunger makes me a very agitated and emotionally unstable person. I experience light-headedness. I lose my attachment to the earth.

The same happens when I don't drink enough water, although the body signs are weaker. Often, I don't remember to drink enough water. When I am preoccupied with the non-essentials of life, I drink only enough to get by and gradually I find myself feeling more and more sluggish and discontented. These are the times where I may be rude or inconsiderate to others creating negative situations. I don't care about the earth or anyone living on it in those moments. It matters not that I have a peaceful philosophy and peaceful intentions. If I desire

Breath, Water, Light

to feel peaceful and centered, I must have food to eat and water to drink. I can see clearly that if the world is to ever be peaceful, every person must have enough food to eat and water to drink.

How fortunate for me that the remedy for my discontent is readily available, and I can return myself to a state of healthy well-being without too much trouble. Once I regain my connection to my body and to the earth, a state of reverence surrounds me, and I feel deeply aware of life. My emotional body is quiet and content. Can you imagine what the energy of the earth would feel like if everyone had enough food to eat and water to drink?

EXERCISES
Exercise 1: Conscious Water Intake

Purpose: I use this exercise: to connect my awareness to the health of my body, to release toxins in my blood, to send my appreciation to the earth for providing water and to add to the thought of every person in the world having a safe water supply.

Timing/Duration: Every time you drink a glass or bottle of water.

Step by Step Instructions:

1. As you are drinking the water, take time to appreciate the gift of water in our lives. How does water affect your well-being? Do you take baths, refreshing showers? Do you swim and

find it invigorating? Do you enjoy the rain, the oceans, the waterfalls?

2. Feel the blood coursing through the veins of your body. Does it flow smoothly? Does it feel heavy? As you are drinking, try to feel the water entering your system and flowing out through your veins into all parts of your body. Don't worry if at first you can't feel your blood flowing through your body. This will happen in a instant and from that point forward, you will know that you are master of your own health and well-being. It is a feeling that must be experienced to be shared.

3. Once you feel like your blood cells are hydrated, you can start to pay attention to the organs in your body and imagine this fresh light blood flowing through them, releasing built up toxins gently and slowly through your urinary tract.

4. Create a vision in your mind representing all beings having a safe and abundant water supply.

Notes/Comments: I believe that when you add conscious thought to the action of drinking a glass of water, or any action for that matter, you strengthen the effects of the thought.

Exercise 2: Cleansing Emotions

Purpose: I use water to help clean up not just my physical self, but also my emotional self. This happens to most of us naturally, without our being aware of it. Adding conscious thought connects you to your emotional state

Breath, Water, Light

and assists with replacing negative thought with a relaxed state of reverence.

Timing/Duration: Every time you take a bath or shower.

Step by Step Instructions:

1. Imagine the water coming out of the shower washing away any negativity that you are carrying around.

2. While in the bath, take conscious breaths and imagine any toxins and negativity turning to sand and falling away from your body. Watch as they go down the drain.

3. As you emerge refreshed, take two or three conscious breaths and say thank you again for the gift of water.

Notes/Comments: Don't be afraid to invent visualizations and rituals of your own. This is half the fun of being master of your goal of creating and maintaining a peaceful state of existence.

Exercise 3: Water and Flow…Connecting Awareness to the Movement of the Body

There is a blissful state of awareness that comes simply from FEELING the movement of our bodies through time and space. When I am in this state of awareness, walking down the street or washing the dishes becomes a full experience of life. In these moments, I demand nothing from others and something like laughter bubbles through my veins.

Purpose: This exercise of the imagination will assist you with connecting more fully with your physical body.

Timing/Duration: Set aside 15 minutes and do this exercise as often as you like.

Step by Step Instructions:

1. Lie down comfortably with arms resting loosely at your sides and your feet uncrossed.

2. Close your eyes and relax your body by taking 3 or 4 conscious breaths.

3. Imagine you have a shadow body lying inside your physical body.

4. While breathing rhythmically, imagine your shadow body sitting up and putting your feet on the floor.

5. Remember, or imagine if you can't remember, what it feels like to stand and feel the weight of your self and the feeling of the floor touching your feet.

6. Paying attention to every step your shadow self is taking, walk over to the sink or refrigerator and imagine pouring a glass of water.

7. Slowly, remembering what it feels like to drink a glass of water, feel the water entering your

system and clearing and cleaning your shadow self. Drink as many glasses as you need to feel completely refreshed.

8. Put the glass down and slowly walk your shadow self back to your physical body (make sure you didn't leave the water running!!). Remember the feeling of your feet touching the floor and the air moving against your skin.

9. Lie down inside your physical body and take a few more centering breaths.

10. Open your eyes, then repeat this activity for real. Does drinking a glass of water hold more substance now? Can you feel your feet on the ground? Do you feel the air on your face as you are moving? Don't despair if you don't notice a difference in the feeling of your movements! Eventually, you will.

Notes/Comments: Remember, being aware of your physical body will help you see where you are feeling at dis-ease. Once you find these places of dis-ease, often you can use your breath and conscious water intake to assist with the healing. Getting a deeper connection with your physical body will also bring you joyful moments in the simplicity of movement, leaving your emotional body refreshed and energetic.

Exercise 4: Watering and Tending the Garden of Thought

I believe that thoughts have weight and substance. The measuring stick for the weight and substance of a thought is the effect it has on our hearts and bodies, on our perceptions and reactions. I believe that most people have the intention to live a good life. Unfortunately, in a society that glorifies suffering, and in fact thrives on suffering (think doctors, pharmaceuticals, lawyers, weapon makers, etc), like weeds in a garden, fear and worrisome thoughts often overtake our ability to see the gifts in our lives. We give energy to the thoughts that we pay attention to; we feed those thoughts and make them grow. Even if you are condemning negative thoughts and actions, you are still giving them energy and increasing their power.

Purpose: This visualization is helpful for reviewing your own thinking and making changes in your belief structures to help you build a beautiful garden of thoughts within your mind.

Timing/Duration: Set aside at least 15 minutes and do this exercise as often as you can.

Step by Step Instructions:

1. Imagine that your mind is a garden with every thought and belief you have as seeds that were planted in the garden of your mind, from birth until now. Negative belief structures are weeds; positive belief structures are flowers and trees.

2. You are the gardener. What does the garden of your mind look like? What thoughts do you have regarding your self? What thoughts do you have about others around you? What thoughts do you have about the world? What do you think others think about you? Write them down so

they become real, so you can see on paper what has been growing in your garden.

3. If your mind is in a complete state of disarray and you feel that it would take you centuries to control all the weeds that you have growing, imagine a big backhoe taking it all out, good and bad. Burn the plants to ashes and spread over the newly cleared ground as fertilizer.

4. Review your list of thoughts. Ask yourself, does this thought give me a sense of peace? Choose which thoughts need to be discarded and visualize yourself in your garden pulling the weeds at the root. From this point forward, pay more attention to the thoughts that enter your mind and the effect the thought has on your state of being. Accepting a negative thought into your mind is planting the seed; stewing over the thought is watering it and making it grow.

5. Seek out thoughts that make you feel loved and worthy of love, and plant as many of them in your mind as possible. Water them by affirming them to your self as often as you need. Make your own presence a beautiful garden that, at the very least, your own self is happy to live in.

Notes/Comments: Every spoken word, every written word, every action, every emotion represent thoughts. Be diligent in the process of monitoring and questioning your thoughts and belief systems. You are the boss of your thinking. It is never too late to accept or reject any thought that has been planted within you. There is a reason that human beings have the capacity to think. In my thinking, this represents free will.

Exercise 5: The Cup of Life and Appreciation

One day as I was walking in the sunshine, I started thinking about the analogy of the half-empty, half-full cup that people use to describe their overall perception of their life. I saw that if each person started filling their cup with things that we all share that give us life, like sunshine, rain, trees, stars, air, plants, nature, then our cups would never be empty. I realized that it is the order in which we perceive the gifts in our lives that dictate our overall happiness and satisfaction with life.

Purpose: When I am feeling sorry for myself for not getting something I thought was important to me, I use this exercise to put my life in perspective.

Timing/Duration: As needed.

Step by Step Instructions:

1. Sit down comfortably with an empty cup and a jug of water.

2. Take three or four centering breaths and think about what you appreciate about your life. In order of importance, write down or state what you appreciate. For each gift in your life, pour water from the jug into your cup. If you have trouble feeling the emotion of appreciation, think of the things in your life that would make

you sad if they were gone. Whether you actually feel the appreciation at the moment, these are the things in your life that you appreciate.

3. Here are some of the things I appreciate in life, just to give you some examples:

- appreciation of the abundance of nature... the sun on my face, the wind against my skin, the beauty of trees
- beings that love me and allow me to love them back
- a roof over my head
- enough food and water to eat and drink
- laughter
- a healthy body
- ability to learn and explore
- beautiful ideas like honor, honesty, kindness and compassion
- activities that I find fun to do
- self-discovery and passion for life
- material goods and belongings
- exciting vacations

4. If your cup becomes full before you are finished, drink the water in the cup and carry on. Do you feel more blessed than when you started? This exercise makes it really hard for me to feel sorry for myself for any length of time. It can be done in your imagination as well.

I stood
amongst the shadows
in the near-darkness.

Lost and alone,
I sank to the ground
holding my head in my hands.

HELP!
I cried out to the emptiness
surrounding me.

A click echoed in the distance
and I raised my head
to see a doorway full of light
streaming to a point near my feet.

I stood up and followed the light.
With each step, one by one,
the shadows disappeared
and with each step, one by one,
hope and love
gradually filled my heart.

LIGHT

Peaceful Intention

Light is the tool I use when I need to find serenity in dealing with situations that I cannot control or change. I use it to assist with healing and protecting myself, and when dancing and playing, to connect the feeling in my heart to my movements. Light is the guiding force that leads me to the experience of unconditional love; what I would imagine as having the experience of heaven right here on earth. It is a tool of the imagination and has been a constant companion to me daily for many years.

How does one imagine light? If you can imagine the light that surrounds a light bulb, you can picture light. This is the generic form of white light. It can be used as a prayer for peace and right-action to occur in any given situation. Once you are comfortable using light in your imagination, you will be able to assign color and intentional energy to light, and use it for play and healing. Because light covers the whole spectrum of existence, having peaceful intentions when working with it is essential for peaceful results to occur.

I have always felt an abundance of loving energy inside me, but relatively few destinations to send it. When I became a mother, I was able to release this loving energy without modifying it or slowing its escape from my heart.

The peace and contentment I felt in those moments far exceeded any other peaceful and pleasant experience that I had previously had. I understood in those moments that having those willing to receive our love was equally as important as giving loving energy.

I wanted to express my loving self in every day moments in life, not just with my children. I realized that I was spending a lot of time being critical of myself and had put many walls up around me so people wouldn't see my softness and vulnerability. I thought that if I was critical of myself, it would protect me from getting hurt. Instead, it prevented me from receiving the love of others, and enabled others to be critical of me as well.

I believe that the tools that we use to protect ourselves, both physical and mental, are the tools that others can use against us. For this reason, I choose to protect myself with light filled with kind and compassionate energy. In my imagination, the energy of kindness and compassion is rose-colored light. When I surround myself with this light, my hope is that others will feel safe around me, and have no need to attack.

The energy of kindness and compassion comes from the heart. The experience of unconditional love is the strength behind kind and compassionate energy. The pathway to the experience of feeling unconditional love is through an open heart. I believe unconditional love exists for anyone that has the intention to seek it out. Similar to sunlight, it shines on rich and poor alike and we need only find our way to our own hearts in order to catch the rays.

Breath, Water, Light

Living with an open heart makes you vulnerable. Being vulnerable makes you lovable and allows others to love you unconditionally. To experience this feeling, we must allow the walls around our hearts to be penetrated.

Living with an open heart is perhaps the most courageous act a human being can do in this day and age. Open-hearted people feel their own pain and the pain of others. Because pain is in abundance in this world, many people choose to keep their hearts closed and live their lives in a shell. While it is true that pain is avoided, in doing so we lose our connection to the world around us. The shell makes us care less about what happens to others, and in turn others care less about us.

Have you ever met or known someone that you thought was incredibly kind and compassionate? Were you fortunate enough to feel the unconditional love from your father or mother, or other guardians? Do you remember how you felt in their presence? Even if the answer is no, the universe can provide you with this feeling. It is up to you to open up space in your heart for the experience.

The following exercises will assist you with healing and reconnecting to your heart, your mind and your body. In my opinion, the ritual of forgiveness is the most important tool for opening the heart and speeding up the healing process.

Exercise 1: A Prayer for Right Action

Purpose: When I am in a situation where I am feeling attacked or controlled and am unable to resolve the problem, I use this exercise to unburden myself from the weight of the situation. I choose to believe that there is a reason for everything and that reason may be beyond my limited understanding of the purpose of my life and the lives of others. Because of this belief, I am able to take my own judgment out of the situation.

Timing/Duration: Whenever you are feeling injured or controlled by something or someone outside of yourself, and you feel there is nothing you can do to correct the situation.

Step by Step Instructions:

1. Sitting or lying comfortably, take three of four centering breaths.

2. Imagine yourself surrounded by white light and then imagine light around the person/subject that is causing you distress.

3. Ask the powers that be for truth and justice in the situation, and for the highest good of all concerned to be the result.

4. Let go of any ideas of how you think the situation should be resolved and let nature do the rest. Follow your intuition and listen to your heart for guidance, and take responsibility for any part that you have played in the disturbance.

Notes/Comments: Picturing light around the situation gives me something tangible to do and I can assign a peaceful intention to the light. I have immense faith in this. Using light as tool for problem resolution has proven to have unusual and somewhat miraculous results. Choosing this reaction frees me up from vengeful behavior, which I believe can only result in more vengeful behavior. It also frees up my heart for forgiveness, which allows me to maximize the feeling of kindness inside me.

I believe true compassion comes from within. It is an energetic quality, not an action or reaction. Sacrifice and suffering are elevated in our social standards. We revere those who sacrifice and those who suffer for what we perceive are the goals of the common good. Some of us run ourselves ragged helping others, often to find that our help is unwanted or unappreciated, or the results of our endeavors often prove to be less than what we had strived for. Cultivating compassionate energy within is an alternate solution to promoting sacrifice and suffering. It heals simply by being present in the world.

Exercise 2: Returning to the Space of your Heart

I believe all emotional events are stored in our hearts. Some events are precious and beautiful and others, like losing a loved one, are painful. If a person has too much pain stored in their hearts, it is a painful place to be and there is a tendency to avoid dealing with the pain. In order to protect your self with kindness and compassion, living from the heart is necessary.

Purpose: I use this exercise to connect to my heart or feeling-center, in order to release past pain and create room for loving thoughts to exist within me. If your imagination still hasn't opened fully, this exercise can be done in any quiet room in your home, representing the space of your heart.

Timing/Duration: Initially, every day for 10 or 15 minutes until you are satisfied with the state of your heart. Afterwards, as needed.

Step by Step Instructions:

1. Sitting or lying comfortably, take 10 deep breaths and breathe in light and energy into the area of your heart.

2. Imagine a room where all the experiences of your heart are stored. Stand at the door of the room and look around. What does it look like? Is it dusty from lack of attention? Is it packed to the brim with hurts and happy experiences that you have stored up from the past? Is it empty and dark?

3. Make your way to the middle of the room; move things if need be. Imagine drawing a sacred circle of space around your self in the middle of the room.

4. Surround your self with candles of light for protection and illumination.

5. This is your space and your responsibility. Start cleaning out the painful experiences that you have been keeping. Imagine that whatever you shine light on in the spirit of forgiveness disappears into

space. Give thanks for the loving experiences that you have had. Your appreciation is like dusting a beautiful antique or piece of art.

6. When you are ready, draw your circle bigger. This circle represents the amount of love you are willing to receive in your day to day life. Pay attention to the windows in the room. If there are none, create some. The light needs to find a way in. Make sure they open so that you can feel the refreshing breeze of loving attention when it comes to you.

7. Receive every bit of appreciation and love for your self graciously. Accepting love is so important, not just for your self, but for the person giving it. We receive what we give so the best gift you can give to another is to receive their love.

8. While you are in this space, you can ask for your own angel or guide to appear before you. A protective angel is worthwhile having through these turbulent times. Ask that negative energies be dispelled at the door. Remember, your heart is precious. I believe it is the connection between your earth life and the life of your soul.

Exercise 3: The Ritual of Forgiveness

The best experiences I have had in life are the times when I am feeling warm and affectionate. I have a limited capacity for holding onto anger and grudges, simply because I don't like the feeling, not because I am saintly in my quest for forgiveness. Holding grudges and hurts within your heart and body is much like creating icebergs within the heart of your physical and emotional self. It makes you a cold person. Forgiveness must start out as an intention, as very few of us have the capacity to truly FEEL like forgiving after being hurt by another. The intention of forgiveness is like the warm wind that starts the melt.

Purpose: I use this exercise to prevent my heart from hardening, so I can enjoy the feeling of being alive. Along with The Prayer for Right Action, I free myself from the controlling behaviors of others, and refuse to become a victim of the suffering of another.

Timing/Duration: Whenever you feel cold and unloving towards your self or others, or daily as needed to maintain kind and compassionate energy inside and around you.

Step by Step Instructions:

1. State your intention to forgive all past and/or present grudges. It can be specific or all encompassing, releasing grudges that you may have forgotten you are holding on to.

2. State that you wish for only the Highest Good of All Concerned.

3. Using your own imagination, assign a physical ritual to your intention of forgiveness. This connects the forgiveness to your concrete senses and puts you in touch with your physical self. This could take the form of a hand movement or

a dance or some ritual you are already doing if you follow a religious belief system.

4. If you are attempting to forgive a specific event, do the Prayer for Right Action and ask for guidance about what you need to do to relieve the grudge. Pay attention and accept the guidance when it arrives. This can come from within as a feeling of knowing or from without, where someone or something outside of your self shows you a sign that touches the core truth of the matter. It is my experience that I have had a part to play in every negative incident that has befallen me. Often I find myself saying sorry within my mind for any part that I played in causing the hurtful behavior.

5. Cry when you need to without feeling weak about it; this is the best sign that ice is in fact melting.

6. Keep to the process at least two or three times past the point where you think nothing is happening and you get sick of doing it. I believe this is actually one of the most important steps because typically ego resistance rises the most when the ice is ready to completely disappear. You may be telling your self that your work is done, when really you have found a different place to hide the hurt.

7. Once you have made more space in your heart, accept the kind and beautiful thoughts that are waiting for you and plant them in the garden of your mind.

Notes/Comments: As your garden of thought grows more and more beautiful, your energy will become more and more beautiful. You will be noticed. Be patient with those around you who aren't used to seeing you this way, and may feel threatened by you standing on your own two feet. Negative patterns can appear to be safety nets to those who would rather evaluate someone else's state of mind and behavior than to address their own issues. At this point, you may have to make some tough decisions as to whom you choose to share your presence with.

Exercise 4: Enhancing the Sacred

If I told you that you were sacred and completely cherished, would you believe it? Most likely not, as most of us have come to associate the sacred with the perfected. I believe that I am sacred, not because of anything I do but because I've experienced unconditional love surrounding me. I am far from perfect so I can only assume that this same kind of feeling can be experienced by anyone that truly wants to experience it. Regardless of your weaknesses and addictions, admitting that you are sacred will gradually show you that everything is sacred and your actions will follow suit.

Each of us is born with gifts and talents. Unfortunately, most of us barely look beneath the surface of our own skin to see what gems we have been given. We compare our selves to others, and most often find ourselves lacking. We must be kind towards our selves over this because we are brainwashed from early on in our life by TV and advertising and social pressures as to what gifts are valuable to have.

Does it make sense that people should consider themselves more valuable and lovable in life than another because of natural talents and gifts? To me, a person should take pride in how they cultivate the gifts and talents they were given, and how willing they are to learn new talents.

Can you imagine what the world would look like and how it would operate if we took comparative thought out of the equation of our self-worth? It seems to be that whoever appears to be getting the most energy from life, be it from fame or wealth, is used as our measuring stick for how well we are doing in this world. How wonderful it would be to have caring, honorable, and respectful behaviors as our measurement tools for what makes a successful life.

Once you have experienced the unconditional love that awaits you, you will never doubt that you are worthy of self-love and self-respect. Be true to your self and strive to live your life in ways that you wish everyone would live their life.

Purpose: I use this exercise to remind myself that I am sacred, unique and special in my own way. When I do this, I am reminded that we are all sacred, unique and special in our own ways.

Timing/Duration: As needed.

Step by Step Instructions:

1. Using your imagination, surround your self with light (in the color that you feel is most sacred).

2. State your intention that you are willing to experience the feeling of unconditional love and to accept that you are sacred and deserve to be treated with respect.

3. Say out loud at least three or four times: I AM SACRED

4. When you greet others or others enter your space, repeat the mantra I AM SACRED within your mind, and while looking at the other person, say within your mind, YOU ARE SACRED. Do this even when you don't believe it. It will take time to overcome years of brainwashing telling you otherwise. Pay attention to the feeling these thoughts have on your experience of life and how others treat you.

5. Sacred space is fun to play with. Once you start, it can get addictive. Whatever you are doing, you can extend your sense of the sacred to everything around you. For example, pretend that everywhere you walk, you create sacred space underneath your feet. Use your imagination as to what this path looks like. Keep this up for a few days, and the pathway from your bedroom to your bathroom will have a completely different feel. Life will regain its mysterious and awe-inspiring status.

6. Another way to extend sacred space is through your hands. Simply tell your hands that they are sacred and that all things that they touch will be blessed by this knowing. There is almost too much

power in these thoughts, especially when you use them when doing the banal tasks, like working on your computer, washing dishes, mowing the lawn, cleaning toilets, changing diapers… anything that would previously seem like work.

Exercise 5: Light and the Dance of Movement

Purpose: I use this exercise to connect my heart to my physical body. Once you have reconnected your awareness to your heart, this exercise will help extend the kind and compassionate energies into the rest of your body. It will open up the energy in your hands in order to be able to share the loving and healing energies that you will be receiving. This exercise increases the joy I feel in movement and strengthens my inner beauty and my desire to express myself from the heart.

Timing/Duration: At least once a week.

Step by Step Instructions:

1. Put on some music that speaks to your heart.

2. Rub your hands together to open up the energy channels.

3. Standing up straight but relaxed, cup your hands in front of your heart. Imagine a column of light descending from the skies straight into your heart.

4. From your heart, imagine the light moving from your heart, through your arms to your hands and

forming a ball of light. The light can be any color you wish.

5. Taking the ball into one hand, make up a hand and arm dance with both arms and hands while feeling the light in your palm, taking care not to drop the ball of light.

6. When you feel the need to change, transfer the ball of light to your other palm, and carry on with the dance. Keep your attention on the ball of light, ensuring that you are aware of its presence at all times.

7. Let your imagination be free, and let your body be moved by the music. Dance with the ball of light between both hands.

8. Allow the light to change shape, expanding and retracting back into a ball. When you are ready, hold your arms up over your head and let the light shower over you, within you and around you. Keep dancing and playing with the light, feeling the energy of the light in all the cells of your body.

Notes/Comments: This exercise can result in a powerful healing awareness if your heart is becoming more open or a wall is removed. Allow yourself an authentic response to the dance. Weep if you need to, laugh if you need to, or just bask in the bliss this dance can bring to you. I believe this dance will have the most amazing affect on men, as many have lost the body-heart connection due to the demands society has made on them.

Every once in a while
I fall in love with myself.
Today, I am my own best friend.
In this space,
it is not hard to brighten the world around me.
People smile at me as I walk by.
I am reflecting the God in all of us.

EPILOGUE

CREATING PEACE USING IMAGINATION

What does a peaceful world look like? Can you imagine it? All inventions and discoveries in the world first started out in someone's imagination. I believe external peace in the world can be invented by individuals collectively using their imagination to create visions of peace.

As a final exercise, I would like you to take the time to imagine what peace looks like to you. Together we can topple the cynicism that has clouded our perceptions and reduce the fear that runs rampant in our lives.

Even if you are unable at the moment to create mental visions of peace, you can put together your own words of what peace looks like. For example, you can say to yourself or write down on paper ideas such as:

'All human beings work together to feed and
    nourish each other'
'All human beings work together to ensure that
    everyone a clean and safe water supply'
'I gladly give of the extra energy and belongings that I
    have to those in need of a level of food and shelter
    that I require to feel safe and comfortable in my life'

Here are some of my visions of what living in a peaceful world looks and feels like:

I am imagining that it's three o'clock in the morning after a blistering hot day. I was restless and could not sleep. I am walking the streets by myself feeling the coolness of the night on my skin, soothing my restless spirit. I feel safe.

I like to picture the soldiers in the world putting down their guns and leaving the game of war. Like a nightmare that ends when one wakes up, they turn away from the fighting and return to their families. Joy at this action surges through them.

In my perfect world, there would be ways to ensure that no person goes hungry, and each soul has protection from the forces of nature. Primary education would be as diligent about teaching kindness and compassion in human relationships and relationships with all creatures of the earth as we are with teaching children reading, writing and arithmetic.

Most importantly, every child would be born out of conscious decision, and loved for simply being, not for performing excellently or looking beautiful. Every child would be of interest to his or her parents and care-givers. The God within would be sought out and adored.

Good luck with your own imaginings of a peaceful world. I hope that one day we will see with our own eyes the visions that we have collectively created joined in love and hope.

I am imagining that you are feeling warm and loved reading these words.

Thank You.

Instructions to a Soldier of Peace

Live by your word.
Live by your honor.
And the strength
of the courageous
will fill your soul.

First…
find your heart,
then follow its truth.
Let this Truth
be your guide
and your companion.

First…
find your heart.
For there are many types of
Truth to follow
in this world.

Only the truth of your heart
will give you the sense of
certainty that is needed
to walk
in your own honor.

Live by your word.
Live by your honor.
Countless gifts will be placed
upon your table.
Clarity of thought,

compassion of heart,
and strength of purpose…
the fuel that transcends time
and brings peace to the troubled.

But first…
find your heart.
Listen for its voice.
Know it, feel it,
Lest you be misled
by the many other voices
clamoring for attention
inside your mind.
Live by your word.
Live by your honor.
Follow your heart and
trust that the path set out
for you
does have a destination
and this destination
reflects peace and truth.

First…
find your heart,
then follow it.
Once you have learned
the ways of your heart,
you will no longer need to
follow it.
You will become it.

You will walk in your word.
You will live in your honor.